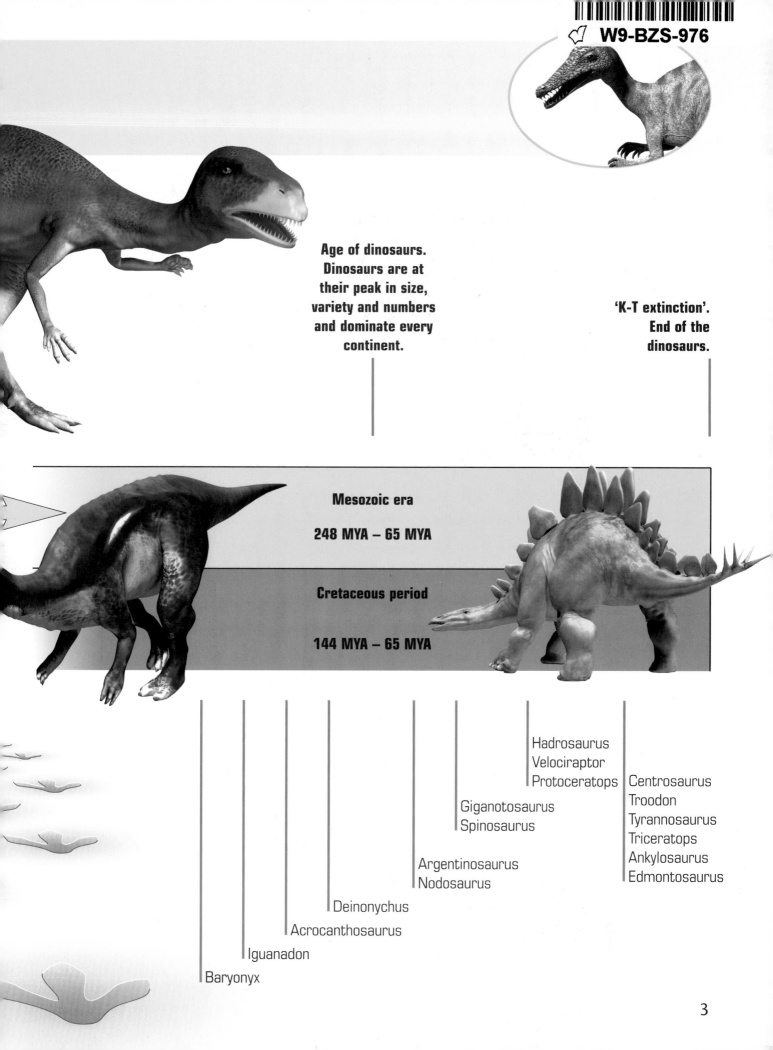

Age of dinosaurs. Dinosaurs are at their peak in size, variety and numbers and dominate every continent.

'K-T extinction'. End of the dinosaurs.

Mesozoic era

248 MYA – 65 MYA

Cretaceous period

144 MYA – 65 MYA

Hadrosaurus
Velociraptor
Protoceratops

Centrosaurus
Troodon
Tyrannosaurus
Triceratops
Ankylosaurus
Edmontosaurus

Giganotosaurus
Spinosaurus

Argentinosaurus
Nodosaurus

Deinonychus

Acrocanthosaurus

Iguanadon

Baryonyx

FULL TIMELINE

Oceans and atmosphere form. Earliest life forms in oceans.

Trilobites dominate seas. Still no land life.

Earliest land plants appear.

Insects flourish. First reptiles evolve. Shrubs, ferns and trees dominate land.

Massive volcanic eruptions cause mass extinctions, wiping out 90% of marine life and 70% of land life!

Precambrian time 4.5–3.9 BYA			Palaeozoic era 540 MYA–248 MYA						
Hadean eon	Archean eon	Proterozoic eon	Cambrian period	Ordovician period	Silurian period	Devonian period	Carboniferous period	Permian period	

The Earth forms!

Sea plants begin photosynthesis.

First fish evolve.

Fish dominate oceans. Spiders and mites are first land creatures. First amphibians evolve. First forests form.

Synapsids, such as Dimetrodon and amphibians such as Eryops dominate land.

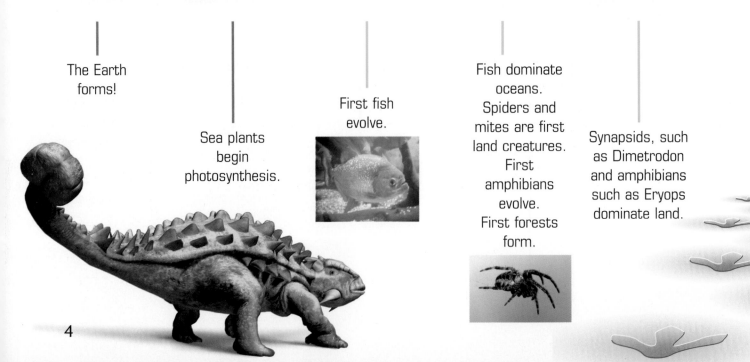

'K-T extinction'
End of the
dinosaurs.

Dinosaurs
dominate.
First mammals
evolve.

Mammals such
as horses, bats
and whales
evolve.

Most modern
birds and
mammals have
evolved.

'Great Ice Age'
Neanderthals and
Homo sapiens, or modern
humans, evolve.
Smilodon (saber-toothed
tiger), mastodons and
mammoths evolve.

Mesozoic era 248 MYA–65 MYA			Cenozoic era 65 MYA–NOW							
			Tertiary period (65 MYA – 1.8MYA)						Quaternary period (1.8MYA – NOW)	
Triassic period	Jurassic period	Cretaceous period	Paleocene epoch	Eocene epoch	Oligocene epoch	Miocene epoch	Pliocene epoch		Pleistocene epoch	Holocene epoch

Creodonts
evolve.
Modern
mammals
become
dominant.

Last ice
age ends.
Human
civilization
develops.

**Age of
dinosaurs.
Dinosaurs are
at their peak in
size, variety and
numbers and
dominate every
continent.**

Sauropsids
such as the
archosaurs
dominate.
First cynodonts
such as
Cynognathus
evolve.
Marine reptiles
evolve.

Mammals
dominate.
Early carnivores
evolve.

Hominids, the
ape-like
ancestors of
humans evolve.
Thylacosmilus
and other early
saber-tooths
evolve.

ICHTHYOSAURUS

Aquatic hunter/killer

FOSSIL FACTS
Ichthyosaurus fossils have been found in England, Germany, Greenland and Canada. The first was found in England in the early 19th century.

Appearance

Ichthyosaurus means 'fish lizard'. It was named in 1818 by Charles König from the British Museum. It is not a true dinosaur but a dolphin-like marine reptile. Ichthyosaurus lived from the early Jurassic period to the early Cretaceous period – around 206 to 140 million years ago.

Ichthyosaurus evolved from reptiles, but could swim like fish. It swam by moving its powerful tails from side to side. Since it needed to breathe air periodically, it probably lived close to the surface of the sea. It breathed through nostrils on the top of the head, near the top of the snout. Its long snout was packed with conical, pointed teeth.

Permian period	Triassic period	Jurassic period	Cretaceous period
(290-248 million years ago)	(248-176 million years ago)	(176-130 million years ago)	(130-66 million years ago)

Reproduction and diet

Ichthyosaurus was smooth-skinned and streamlined, and had limbs (flippers) like large paddles to balance it in the water – the front 'paddles' were twice as large as the back ones. Its eyes were unusually large, and surrounded by a strong ring of bone. A fish-like tail helped propel it, and a dorsal fin provided extra balance.

Ichthyosaurus gave birth to live young – we know this because fossils have been found showing baby Ichthyosaurus bones in the abdomen of adults. Fossils have also helped us learn about the diet of Ichthyosaurus – the hard hooks found on the tentacles of squid cannot be digested and so remained in the belly; one fossil of an Ichthyosaurus showed it had swallowed at least 1,500 squid while alive.

The first complete ichthyosaurus fossil remains were found at Lyme Regis in England, by a girl called Mary Anning, in the early 19th century. Mary Anning made a living from collecting, studying and selling fossils.

MEGA FACTS

- Most were around 6 ft long, though some were as big as 30 ft. An average weight for these dolphin-like creatures was 200 lb.

- We know Ichthyosaurus must have moved fast to hunt its prey, because the remains of a fast-swimming fish called Pholidophorus have been found in fossilized Ichthyosaurus droppings. It could swim at speeds of up to 25 mph.

- Ichthyosaurus skeletons found at Holzmaden, Germany were so well preserved that scientists could see outlines of skin as well as bones.

- In 2000, an Ichthyosaurus skeleton, believed to be almost a perfect specimen, was revealed as a fake when it was cleaned. It had been made in the Victorian age from the bones of two different creatures and some bones made out of plaster.

Icthyosaurus fossil

Dinosaur Data

PRONUNCIATION:	Ik-THEE-OH-**SAWR**-US
SUBORDER:	ICHTHYOSAURIA
FAMILY:	ICHTHYOSAURIDAE
DESCRIPTION:	OCEAN-DWELLING PREDATOR
FEATURES:	ENORMOUS EYES, FOUR CRESCENT-SHAPED FLIPPERS, DORSAL FIN
DIET:	FISH, OCTOPUS AND OTHER

ELASMOSAURUS

Long-necked marine reptile

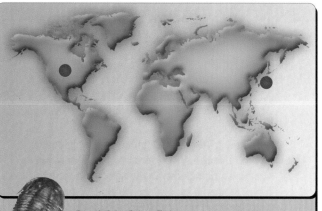

FOSSIL FACTS
Elasmosaurus fossils have been found in North America and Japan. The first was found in 1868.

Elasmosaurus means 'thin-plated lizard' — the name refers to the plate-like bones in the creature's pelvic girdle. It lived 88–65 million years ago, and swam in the great inland sea that covered much of the western part of North America in those times. Its body was dwarfed by its long thin neck and shorter tail.

Elasmosaurus was named by Edward Drinker Cope, who discovered the first fossil.

Unfortunately, when Cope assembled his Elasmosaurus skeleton for display, he placed the head on the wrong end! His rivals soon pointed out his mistake, and made fun of him for it for the rest of his career.

Appearance

The neck of Elasmosaurus contained more than 70 vertebrae. Elasmosaurus was the largest of a type of marine reptile called plesiosaurs. It had a large body, four long, broad paddles for limbs, and a small head with sharp, interlocking teeth.

The long neck may have enabled Elasmosaurus to feed in a number of different ways.

Dinosaur Data

PRONUNCIATION:	EE-**LAZ**-MOH-SAWR-US
SUBORDER:	PLESIOSAURIOID
FAMILY:	ELASMOSAURIDAE
DESCRIPTION:	HUGE, SLOW-SWIMMING MARINE REPTILE
FEATURES:	EXTREMELY LONG NECK, TINY HEAD
DIET:	FISH AND OTHER SMALL MARINE CREATURES

It may have floated along on the surface, stretching down to the sea bottom to catch fish and other marine creatures. It could also make attacks upward at shoals of fish while its body was much lower down in the water. It could move slowly and stealthily toward them, then attack with a quick darting movement. The small size of its head and its narrow neck meant it could only eat and swallow smaller creatures. Elasmosaurus fossils have been found with rounded pebbles in their stomachs – perhaps they swallowed these to aid their digestion or to help them sink further down into the water.

Elasmosaurus is believed to have been a very slow swimmer. It would have traveled long distances to find safe mating and breeding grounds.

Reproduction

For a long time, it was assumed that Elasmosaurus laid eggs like most reptiles, crawling ashore to lay its eggs on land. However, many scientists now think that Elasmosaurus gave birth to live young, which it raised until they could look after themselves in the predator-filled ocean. Elasmosaurus may have traveled together in small groups to protect their young.

MEGA FACTS

- About 46 ft long, Elasmosaurus was the longest of the plesiosaurs.

- Pictures often show Elasmosaurus holding its head high above the surface of the water at the end of its long neck. Actually, gravity would have made it impossible for it to lift much more than its head above water.

- Elasmosaurus, with its long snake-like neck, is one of the candidates for the Loch Ness Monster.

KRONOSAURUS

Giant short-necked marine reptile

D I N O S A U R S   I N   T H E   S E A

Kronosaurus means 'Kronos's lizard'. It had a short neck, four flippers, a huge head with powerful jaws and a short, pointed tail.

Kronosaurus was a marine reptile called a pliosaur (a type of plesiosaur). It was heavier, faster and fiercer than most plesiosaurs. It lived in the seas that covered parts of Australia, and breathed air. It swam with four powerful paddle-like flippers and may have been able to climb out onto land and move around a little. It probably had to leave water to lay its eggs in nests it would dig in the sand.

Diet

Kronosaurus ate other sea creatures such as ammonites and squid. Rounded teeth at the back of its powerful jaws enabled Kronosaurus to crunch up tough shells and crush bone.

The fossilized remains of turtles and even smaller plesiosaurs have been found in the stomachs of Kronosaurus fossils, and long-necked plesiosaur skeletons have been found with Kronosaurus-like toothmarks on the bones. Like Elasmosaurus, small stones have been found in Kronosaurus stomachs which might have helped them grind up their food during digestion.

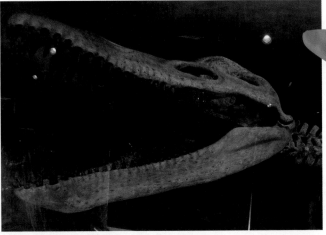

Kronosaurus skeleton

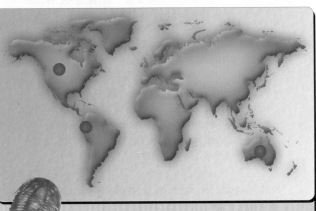

FOSSIL FACTS
Kronosaurus fossils have been found in Australia and Columbia – the first were found in Queensland, Australia by A. Crombie in 1889.

Kronosaurus

Dinosaur Data

PRONUNCIATION:	CROW-NO-SAWR-US
DESCRIPTION:	POWERFUL AQUATIC PREDATOR
FEATURES:	HUGE HEAD, POWERFUL JAWS
DIET:	**CARNIVORE**; ATE OTHER MARINE CREATURES

Kronosaurus may have been able to 'scent' under water for its prey – it had internal nostrils where water could enter, and external ones further back on the top of its skull for water to exit. While the water passed from one set to the other, scent particles could be detected.

Appearance

Kronosaurus had an enormous head as skulls have been found measuring 10 ft. As their whole body length is believed to be only around 30 ft,

MEGA FACTS

- Fast and fierce – one of the top predators of the ancient ocean.

- Some of Kronosaurus' teeth were 10 in. long, although much of this length was embedded in the jawbone.

- When Kronosaurus fossils were first discovered in 1889, they were believed to come from an ichthyosaur. Kronosaurus did not get a name of its own until 1924.

- When the first Kronosaurus skeleton was assembled, the specimen was in such a bad state that the team had to fill in many details using plaster and their own imagination. This led to the creature being nicknamed the 'Plasterosaurus'!

this means their head took up a third of it!

It was originally thought to be much longer, earning it the title of 'largest ever plesiosaur', but recent studies have led scientists to downsize their image of Kronosaurus. The team of scientists who mounted the first specimen for display had to fill in many 'gaps' in the skeleton – they gave their mounted Kronosaurus too many vertebrae and so made it longer than it should have been.

11

TYLOSAURUS

Gigantic marine predator

DINOSAURS IN THE SEA

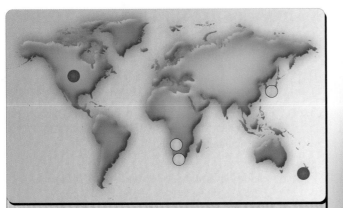

FOSSIL FACTS

Tylosaurus fossils have been found in North America and New Zealand. The first fossils were found in Kansas in 1869. The yellow dots show where material which may relate to Tylosaurus has also been found – in Angola, South Africa and Japan.

The name Tylosaurus comes from the Greek words *tylos* (knob or protuberance) and *sauros* (lizard). It is named for its remarkable long and almost cylindrical snout that has a rounded, bony end. Tylosaurus was a marine reptile known as a mosasaur. It was one of the most gigantic of the mosasaurs, growing up to 39 ft long – that's as long as a bus!

Dinosaur Data

PRONUNCIATION:	**TIE**-LOW-**SAWR**-US
SUBORDER:	LACERTILIA
FAMILY:	MOSASAURIDAE
DESCRIPTION:	MASSIVE SEA PREDATOR
FEATURES:	POWERFUL TAIL, LONG ROUNDED SNOUT
DIET:	FISH, MARINE CREATURES, FLIGHTLESS BIRDS

Appearance

It had a long slender body with a long and powerful tail to propel it through the water. Most scientists think it propelled itself by moving its tail from side to side, just as a crocodile does. It had a long and massive head which was over 3 ft long. Its four limbs were long, slim flippers. The bony tip at the end of its long narrow snout may have been used to ram and stun its prey, and to fight with other Tylosaurus. Its huge jaws contained masses of sharp cone-shaped teeth.

Like most mosasaurs, Tylosaurus probably had a forked tongue, the ability to 'smell' scent particles in water or air (like snakes), and large eyes (and, so, excellent eyesight).

MEGA FACTS

- Tylosaurus rarely bit off more than it could chew – it was able to flex its lower jaw, allowing it to open its mouth very wide and swallow large prey in one piece, just like a modern snake.

- In 2002, a Tylosaurus skeleton went on display at the Alabama Museum of Natural History. It took an estimated 2,000 hours of work to recover and prepare this specimen.

- Tylosaurus not only had a bony bump on the end of its snout, but bony plates on its head and scales all over its body.

Diet

These giant sea hunters ate other sea creatures – fish, shellfish, smaller mosasaurs, turtles and even diving pterandons that dipped too close to the sea's surface!

Many different species of Tylosaurus have been named over the years, but scientists now recognize only a handful as valid. These are:

- Tylosaurus proriger
- Tylosaurus nepaeolicius
- Tylosaurus haummuriensis
- Tylosaurus kansasensis

MOSASAURUS

Giant aquatic predator

DINOSAURS IN THE SEA

Mosasaurus is named after the River Meuse near Maastricht (Netherlands), where the first fossil specimen was found (*mosa-*, the Latin name for the Meuse River, and *-saurus* for lizard). It was given this name in 1822.

Mosasaurus was a gigantic meat-eating reptile that lived 70–65 million years ago. It frequented shallow seas, as it still needed to breathe air. It had a long, streamlined body, four paddle-like limbs, and a long, powerful tail. It was a powerful swimmer, between 39 ft and 58 ft in length. Its large head had huge jaws (up to 5 ft long). These jaws could open up to 3 ft thanks to the Mosasaurus' peculiar jaw design.

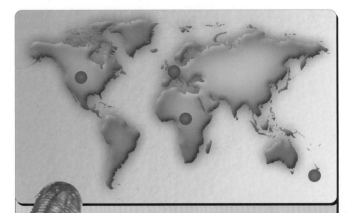

Dinosaur Data

PRONUNCIATION:	**MOES**-AH-**SAWR**-US
DESCRIPTION:	GIANT, SWIFT-MOVING AQUATIC PREDATOR
FEATURES:	SPECIALLY HINGED JAWS, LONG AND POWERFUL TAIL
DIET:	SHARKS, FISH AND OTHER MARINE REPTILES

FOSSIL FACTS

Fossils have been found in North America, Africa, New Zealand and Europe. The first Mosasaurus fossil was found in a quarry in the Netherlands in 1780.

Jaws

Mosasaurus had very special jaws. It had an extra joint halfway along the jaw, which let it handle huge mouthfuls of food. Its lower jaw could drop lower and also move out sideways – much like snakes which can 'unhinge' their jaws to swallow very large pieces of food like whole rats. Monitor lizards, to which Mosasaurus is directly related, still has this special jaw. Set into this jaw were rows of backward-curving teeth. Just as with sharks, when one tooth wore down, another grew in its place.

Diet

The preserved stomach contents of Mosasaur fossils show them to have eaten sharks, bony fish, turtles and other marine reptiles.

Skeleton

Mosasaurus had about 100 vertebrae in its back (four times as many as humans), each joined to the next by a flexible ball-and-socket joint. This would have allowed Mosasaurus to move in the water like an eel. It was one of the most ferocious aquatic predators of its time.

Reproduction

Scientists cannot agree as to whether Mosasaurus came up on land to lay its eggs in sand (like turtles), or gave birth to live young in the water.

Mosasaurus fossils were some of the earliest dinosaur fossils to be discovered, and because of them, scientists began to discuss the possibility that such fossils belonged to species which had actually died out.

MEGA FACTS

- Mosasaurus is directly related to monitor lizards.

- Recent studies suggest the first Mosasaurus specimen was actually a partial skull found as early as 1766, near St Pietersburg, near Maastricht.

- In 1795, a Mosasaurus skull was traded to the occupying French army for 600 bottles of wine! It sits in a Paris museum.

- Like a Tylosaurus, a Mosasaurus rarely bit off more than it could chew – it could unhinge its special jaw to swallow huge prey such as sharks.

Mosasaurus skeleton

15

OPHTHALMOSAURUS

Huge-eyed aquatic hunter

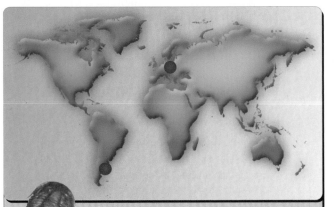

FOSSIL FACTS
Fossils have been found in Europe and Argentina. The earliest find was made by British scientist Harry Seeley in 1874.

Ophthalmosaurus means 'eye lizard' in Greek. The name comes from its dinner-plate sized eyes – Ophthalmosaurus had the largest eyes relative to its size of any vertebrate, measuring up to

9 in. across. These eyes took up almost the whole depth of its skull on each side. Fossil remains show a ring of strong bone surrounding these eyes – these would have supported the eye against water pressure, suggesting that Ophthalmosaurus could dive into deep, dark water after prey or to hide from predators.

It may well have been a night hunter, as its large eyes were well adapted for low light conditions and would have helped it to spot the squid that were its favorite prey. (Large eyes can house more light-gathering cells, and so are more effective in the dark.)

Appearance

Although it was perfectly adapted for living in the water, Ophthalmosaurus needed to breathe air, like a dolphin or whale does. It was not a true dinosaur,

Dinosaur Data

PRONUNCIATION:	OFF-**THAL**-MOH-**SAW**-RUS
FAMILY:	ICHTHYSAURIDAE
DESCRIPTION:	DOLPHIN-LIKE HUNTER
FEATURES:	ENORMOUS EYES
DIET:	SQUID AND FISH

DINOSAURS IN THE SEA

but a marine reptile. Swift and supple, its 20 ft long body resembled that of a dolphin, tear-shaped with a dorsal fin. Its front fins were more developed than its back ones; Ophthalmosaurus probably propelled itself with its tail and steered with its front fins. The skull took up about 3 ft of its 20 ft body.

The bends

Although it could dive to great depths, Ophthalmosaurus may have paid a price for doing so. Fossil evidence shows clear signs of what modern deep-sea divers call the bends – when a diver ascends too quickly, decompressed nitrogen in the blood forms painful bubbles that can damage tissue and even bone. Ophthalmosaurus remains show signs of the animal having suffered in exactly this way, leaving visible depressions in the joints and limb bones.

Reproduction

Ophthalmosaurus could not get onto land to lay eggs, instead giving birth to live young in the water. Their young – which we call 'pups' – were born tail first, to prevent them from drowning. We know this because fossils survive of females in the act of giving birth. Numbers of young ranged from two to 11, although it seems to have been most normal to give birth to only two or three at a time.

Ophthalmosaurus and Stenosaurus

MEGA FACTS

- Ophthalmosaurus lived 165–150 million years ago.

- May have been capable of diving to depths of 3 miles; calculations show it would still have had clear sight this far down.

- Had an almost toothless jaw, specially adapted for catching squid and fish.

17

PLESIOSAURUS

Four-paddled marine reptile

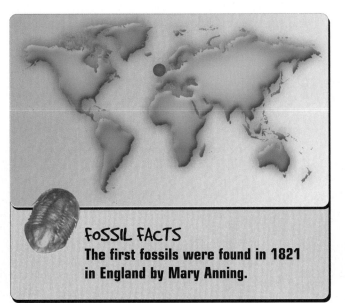

FOSSIL FACTS
The first fossils were found in 1821 in England by Mary Anning.

Plesiosaurus skeleton

The name Plesiosaurus means 'near to lizard' or 'near lizard' and comes from the Greek words *plesios* (near to) and *sauros* (lizard). The name was coined by H. T. De La Beche and William D. Conybeare in 1821.

Appearance

Plesiosaurus was one of a number of marine reptiles that lived at the same time as the dinosaurs. Plesiosaurus was characterized by a long, thin neck, tiny head and a wide body. Plesiosaurus was about 7 ft 6 in. long and may have weighed around 198 lb.

Plesiosaurus lived in the open oceans but still needed to breathe air, this means it would had to have come to the surface regularly to breathe – much like whales and dolphins do.

We believe it swam using its four flippers in pairs, one pair 'rowing' and the other pair moving in an up-down motion with the tail being used for steering. No other creatures are known to swim in this way.

Reproduction

Scientists had speculated that, like the turtle, it dragged itself up onto sandy beaches to lay its eggs, which it would bury in the sand before heading back to the ocean again.

However, the current theory is that the Plesiosaurus gave birth to live young in the oceans. This would certainly have made things easier on the baby Plesiosaurus as it wouldn't have to hatch and then scurry down the beach to reach the relative safety of the ocean like baby sea turtles.

Diet

Fossilized remains found in the stomachs of Plesiosaurus fossils show that they ate fish and other swimming animals. We know they also swallowed small stones! We believe this was either to help to break up their food or to help weight them down for diving deeper into the ocean.

The first Plesiosaurus fossils were found on the Jurassic Coast. In 2004 a fully intact fossilized juvenile Plesiosaurus was found about 31 miles north of where the first Plesiosaurus was found!

DINOSAURS IN THE SEA

18

MEGA FACTS

- The first Plesiosaurus fossil was found long before the first dinosaur fossil was found.

- A Plesiosaurus is one of the creatures mentioned in Jules Verne's *Journey to the Centre of the Earth* – it battles an Icthyosaur.

- Many people believe that the Loch Ness Monster could be a Plesiosaurus. However, this seems unlikely as the cold water of the loch would not support a cold-blooded creature like the Plesiosaurus and the loch only formed 10,000 years ago – while Plesiosaurus became extinct millions of years ago.

Dinosaur Data

PRONUNCIATION:	**PLEE**-SEE-O-**SAWR**-UHS
SUBORDER:	PLESIOSAUROID
FAMILY:	PLESIOSAURIDAE
DESCRIPTION:	ROUGHLY MAN-SIZED AQUATIC PREDATOR
FEAUTURES:	LONG SINUOUS NECK, FOUR PADDLE-LIKE FINS, TINY HEAD WITH LONG SHARP TEETH
DIET:	FISH AND SMALLER AQUATIC ANIMALS

NOTHOSAURUS

Paddle-limbed marine reptile

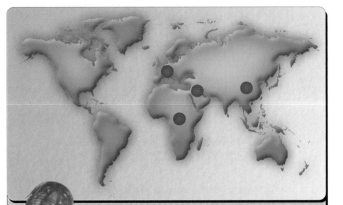

FOSSIL FACTS
Fossils have been found in Europe, the Middle East, Asia and Africa.

interlocking teeth acted like a trap for fish – once it got a grip, Nothosaurus did not easily let go.

Powerful legs and a strong tail made Nothosaurus a very strong swimmer. Although it certainly hunted its food in the water, Nothosaurus probably did not live in the water all the

Nothosaurus means 'false lizard'. It was not a dinosaur at all, in spite of its lizard-like appearance. It is one of a whole group of reptiles called nothosaurs. This group was named by G. von Meunster in 1834.

Nothosaurs

Nothosaurs were long-tailed and long-necked fish-eating marine reptiles. They covered an incredible range of sizes, from less than 8 in. to 20 ft long! All of them had four broad, paddle-shaped limbs, probably with webbed fingers and toes. They had long necks, a narrow head with long, thin snouts and nostrils on top so they could breathe while swimming. They may have also had a fin on their tails to help them steer in the water.

It is difficult to give a 'typical' size for this marine reptile, since we know of at least eight different species of Nothosaurus. Between 3 and 10 ft is probably correct.

In its mouth were fang-like teeth that pointed outwards, suggesting its main diet was fish. Smaller teeth lined its jaws all the way to the back of its cheeks. Its sharp,

Dinosaur Data

PRONUNCIATION:	NO-THO-**SAWR**-US
SUBORDER:	NOTHOSAURIA
FAMILY:	NOTHOSAURIDAE
DESCRIPTION:	FISH-EATING MARINE REPTILE
FEATURES:	PADDLE-LIKE LIMBS, LONG POINTED TAIL
DIET:	FISH AND SHRIMP

time like its descendants the later plesiosaurs. It would have come up onto rocks and beaches, just like a seal, to rest. Scientists believe it also came up on land to lay its eggs. Many fossils of young Nothosaurus have been discovered in what were caves during the Triassic period. Few creatures at that time lived in caves, making them a safe place for the eggs.

MEGA FACTS

- Scientists have found at least eight different kinds of Nothosaur.

- Nothosaurs went extinct during the late Triassic period. They may have evolved into the plesiosaurs.

- Primitive dinosaurs like Lesothosaurus and Herrerasaurus were just beginning to appear on earth at the time Nothosaurus lived.

DIMORPHODON

Primitive fish-eating winged reptile

FOSSIL FACTS
Fossils have been found in England. The first fossils were found by Mary Anning near Lyme Regis in 1828.

The name Dimorphodon means 'two-form teeth'. It was named by palaeontologist Sir Richard Owen in 1859. It has two distinct kinds of teeth – those at the front are longer than those at the back.

Appearance

Dimorphodon was actually a winged reptile called a pterosaur that lived at the same time as the dinosaurs. It is one of the earliest pterosaurs that have been discovered, living 206–180 million years ago, and quite a small one at 3 ft long. Its wings were formed by a leathery membrane which stretched between its body, the top of its legs and its fourth finger. Its hollow bones made it light in the air.

It had a massive head, with wide and deep jaws. The head was extremely large compared to the rest of the body, and it is thought the large beak may have been colored, making it useful for display to other Dimorphodons. Like all pterosaurs, it had huge eyes and, so, probably excellent eyesight.

At the other end of its body was a long, pointed tail, which ended in a curious diamond-shaped flap of skin. This tail may have helped stabilize the creature while in the air, or helped to balance it while walking on the ground.

Dinosaur Data

PRONUNCIATION:	DIE-**MORF**-OH-DON
SUBORDER:	RHAMPHORYNCHOIDEA
FAMILY:	DIMORPHODONTIDAE
DESCRIPTION:	PRIMITIVE WINGED REPTILE
FEATURES:	TWO DIFFERENT KINDS OF TEETH IN ITS BEAK
DIET:	FISH, INSECTS AND POSSIBLY SMALL ANIMALS

FLYING DINOSAURS

MEGA FACTS

- It had a wingspan of 6 ft.

- The specimen found by Mary Anning is believed to have been the first complete pterosaur skeleton ever discovered.

- It may have used its increased leg span to hold onto cliffs while waiting for fish to surface – then swooped down to catch its next meal.

How it moved

There is disagreement about how Dimorphodon moved when it was not flying. Fossil tracks seem to suggest that it went on all fours, but some scientists think it was capable of standing fully or semi-upright on its hind legs and even running quite fast. Unlike most other pterosaurs, Dimorphodon had legs which rather stuck out to the sides, which would have given it a somewhat clumsy, waddling gait. This leads some palaeontologists to suggest it may have spent most of its time off the ground, hanging from tree branches or cliffs, using its grasping hands and toe claws to hold on.

It has often been thought that Dimorphodon would have been able to run very fast, rising up onto its toes to do so. Recently-discovered fossil evidence, though, suggests that it was actually incapable of bending its foot – it would have been flat-footed and needed to place either all or none of its foot on the ground.

Dimorphodon skull

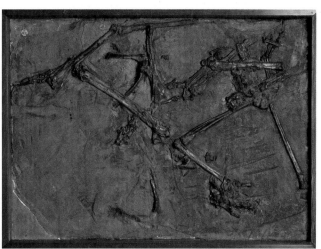

Dimorphodon fossilized skeleton

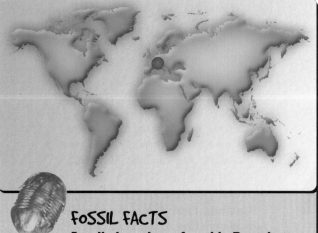

ARCHAEOPTERYX

Winged and feathered bipedal carnivore

FOSSIL FACTS
Fossils have been found in Bavaria, in Germany.

Bird-like features	Dinosaur-like features
Feathered wings with reduced finger	Claws on wings, could be used to grasp
Wishbone	Teeth
Bird-like brain	Long bony tail
Hollow bones	Jaws (not a beak!)
Feathers on body and tail	

This table gives details of the features that Archaeopteryx shared with birds and dinosaurs.

In 2004, an experiment was carried out at the National History Museum in London to try to answer this question. Scanning equipment was used to scan the brain case of an Archaeopteryx skull. The brain shape was much more like that of a modern bird than the brain of a dinosaur.

Archaeopteryx means 'ancient feather'. It was named by Hermann von Meyer in 1861. Archaeopteryx is often said to be a link between dinosaurs and birds.

Appearance

Archaeopteryx was magpie-sized, weighing around 12 oz. It had short, broad wings and a long tail and neck. Its jaws were lined with sharp cone-shaped teeth. It had long legs, with long thighs and short calves. Its wings, body and tail were feathered. Its large eyes would have given it excellent vision. It had feathers and wings like a bird, but teeth, skeleton and claws like a dinosaur.

In 2005, a particularly well-preserved fossil specimen was studied. The second toe could be stretched much more than the rest, rather like the special 'retractable' claws of Velociraptor. The hind toe was not 'reversed' like a thumb on a grasping hand, and so Archaeopteryx could not have used it to cling onto branches.

Could Archaeopteryx fly?

Scientists have argued over whether or not this animal could fly ever since the first Archaeopteryx fossil was found. If it could fly, did it just flap its wings weakly, or fly strongly?

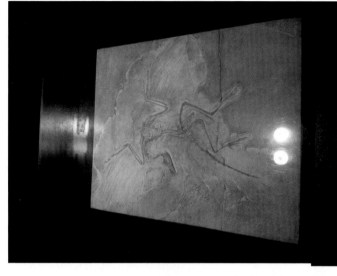

Archaeopteryx fossil

MEGA FACTS

- Only ten Archaeopteryx fossils exist, and only one feather sample.

- Archaeopteryx's brain was only the size of a conker. But the size of its brain compared to its body was three times as big as that of similar sized reptiles.

- It had a wingspan of 18 in.

- There were flying dinosaurs before and after Archaeopteryx, but they had skin, not feathers, on their wings.

The areas controlling vision and movements were enlarged, just like a bird's, and the inner ear (which controls balance) was also like a bird's. It was a brain designed for flight and balance!

Dr Angela Milner, who carried out the study, believes this is strong evidence that Archaeopteryx could and did fly. Most scientists now agree that archaeopteryx *could* fly, but was a weak flyer.

Dinosaur Data

PRONUNCIATION:	ARK-EE**OP**-TER-IKS
SUBORDER:	THERAPODA
FAMILY:	ARCHAEOPTERIDAE
DESCRIPTION:	FEATHERED BIPEDAL CARNIVORE
FEATURES:	FEATHERED WINGS
DIET:	INSECTS, SMALL CREATURES

PTERANODON INGENS

Winged and toothless flying reptile

FLYING DINOSAURS

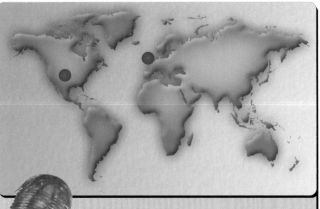

It probably looked more like a huge bat than a bird with large soft hair covered membranes for wings. The membrane itself was very thin but extremely strong and stretched out between the body and the tops of its legs. These flying reptiles did not have any feathers.

FOSSIL FACTS
Fossils have been found in the USA and in England. The first was found in 1876.

Dinosaur Data

PRONUNCIATION:	TER-AN-O-DON
SUBORDER:	PTERODACTYLOIDEA
FAMILY:	PTERADONTIDAE
DESCRIPTION:	CARNIVORE
FEATURES:	HUGE WINGSPAN
DIET:	FISH, MOLLUSCS, CRABS, INSECTS

Pteranodon lived at the same time as Tyrannosaurus Rex. It was not a true dinosaur but was related to them.

Pteranodon had a wing span of up to 30–33 ft and weighed around 44–55 lb.

It would have been able to walk on the ground but, once in the air, Pteranodon would have looked like a huge glider. Pteranodon could fly long distances using its large light-weight wings; it would have taken advantage of rising thermals to soar over the swampy forest below.

MEGA FACTS

- It used the large bony crest on its head to steer when flying.

- Their brightly-colored crests were larger in the male and were used for attracting females and indicating readiness to mate.

- Their lower jaw was over 3 ft in length.

- They would have been agile, elegant and quite fast when flying, reaching speeds up to 30 mph.

Diet

It had no teeth but was carnivorous. Fossil skeletons found near the edge of the sea show that fish was probably an important part of its diet. Its scoop-like beak would have helped it to swoop down to catch fish straight from near the surface of the water. Its excellent eyesight would have helped it to see fish in the water as it flew above the surface.

RHAMPHORYNCUS

Flying reptile

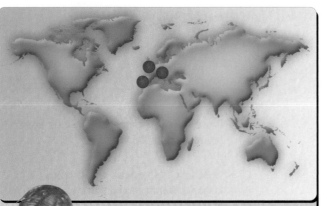

Rhamphorhynchus also had long and thin jaws with incredibly sharp teeth, probably for catching fish. It is believed that one of the ways Rhamphorhynchus hunted was by dragging its beak in the water in the hope of coming into contact with fish, then it would snap its needle-sharp teeth shut and toss the food into its throat pouch. It probably wouldn't have hunted on land as it only had tiny legs, which would have made it a poor runner.

FOSSIL FACTS

Fossils of both these dinosaurs have been found in England, Germany and Portugal. The most detailed were found in Bavaria, southern Germany and show impressions of soft tissues such as the wings and tail.

Rhamphorhynchus was a pterosaur, which lived during the late Jurassic period. It had a wingspan up to 6 ft. The wings were made of thin skin stretched between an elongated finger from its hand, down to its ankle.

Rhamphorhynchus had a long, thin and pointed tail. At the end of its tail it had a flap of skin, which was diamond shaped. This helped with its balance in flight.

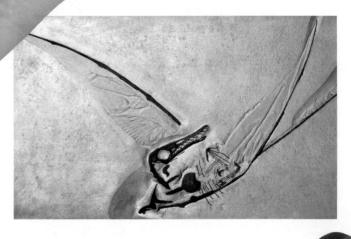

Dinosaur Data

PRONUNCIATION:	**RAM**-FOR-**INK**-US
SUBORDER:	RHAMPHORHYNCHOIDEA
FAMILY:	RHAMPHORHYNCHIDAE
DESCRIPTION:	FLYING REPTILE
FEATURES:	BIRD-LIKE MEAT EATER
DIET:	FISH, MOLLUSKS, INSECTS

PTEROSAUR

Flying reptile

Dinosaur Data

PRONUNCIATION:	TER-OH-**SAW**
SUBORDER:	PTERODACTYLOIDEA
FAMILY:	PTEROSAUR
DESCRIPTION:	FLYING REPTILES
FEATURES:	BIRD-LIKE MEAT EATERS
DIET:	FISH, MOLLUSKS, INSECTS

MEGA FACTS

- Pterosaur bones were hollow, just like those of birds.

- Pterosaurs had large brains and good eyesight.

- Some pterosaurs were covered in a type of hair, or fibers.

- Competition with early bird species may have resulted in the extinction of many of the Pterosaurs.

Pterosaurs were flying reptiles and they lived from the late Triassic period to the end of the Cretaceous period, 228 to 65 million years ago. Pterosaurs were the first vertebrates that were able to fly. When Pterosaurs were first discovered, it was thought that they lived in water. However, in the 19th century Georges Cuvier proposed that pterosaurs flew.

Pterosaur wings were covered with a tough and leathery membrane that stretched between its body, the top of its legs and its fourth finger.

There were many different types of pterosaurs and their wing designs differed. This meant that some of the species flapped their wings and could fly with great power. Others simply glided through the air, relying on updrafts of warm air to help them fly.

Quite a few species of pterosaurs had webbed feet, which could have been used for swimming, but some believe that they were used to help gliding pterosaurs.

When the great extinction wiped out all the dinosaurs at the end of the Cretaceous period, the pterosaurs also disappeared.

29

QUETZALCOATLUS

Feathered serpent god

Living at the same time as Tyrannosaurus Rex and Triceratops it would have been an impressive sight as it swooped down low over the swampy wetlands of the southern US scavenging for food. Its enormous size made it four times larger than today's scavenging birds, the condors and vultures.

Its outstretched neck was 10 ft long with a slim, pointed toothless beak 6 ft long. On the top of its head was a short, bony crest. At the front of its wings were small three fingered hands equipped with sharp claws. Swept behind it as it flew were its vast feet – each larger than an adult human's leg.

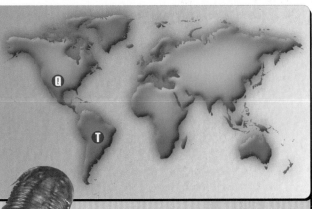

FOSSIL FACTS
Quetzalcoatlus fossils have been found in Texas. Tropeognathus fossils, discovered in rocks in the Santana Formation in north-eastern Brazil have been very precisely dated to 115 million years ago.

Quetzalcoatlus was named in 1975 after the Aztec feathered serpent god, although Quetzalcoaltus itself probably didn't have any feathers, just fine fur like a bat.

As with other pterasaurs, and birds today, its hollow bones would have helped it to fly and remain airborne despite its vast size. Using rising thermals to soar through the air, Quetzalcoatlus would have fed on fish or scavenged on rotting carcasses it found around the water's edge.

With a wingspan of 39 ft, maybe more, it was one of the largest flying animals ever to have lived. It would have weighed around 154 lb – the same sort of weight as an adult human.

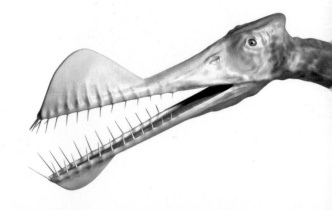